Made in the USA
Middletown, DE
19 May 2020

95438325R00064